Floriography Child

ALSO BY LISA C. KRUEGER

Rebloom

animals the size of dreams

Talisman

Run Away to the Yard

history beyond honeysuckle

Through Rampant Trees

Still Life/Life Still

Floriography Child

a memoir in poems

LISA C. KRUEGER

Red Hen Press | Pasadena, CA

Book design by Mark E. Cull.

Library of Congress Cataloging-in-Publication Data

Names: Krueger, Lisa C., author.
Title: Floriography child: memoir / Lisa C. Krueger.
Other titles: Floriography child (Compilation)
Description: First edition. | Pasadena, CA: Red Hen Press, [2023]
Identifiers: LCCN 2022057023 (print) | LCCN 2022057024 (ebook) | ISBN
   9781636281100 (hardcover) | ISBN 9781636281483 (tradepaper) | ISBN
   9781636281117 (ebook)
Subjects: LCGFT: Autobiographical poetry. | Essays. | Art.
Classification: LCC PS3611.R84 F58 2023 (print) | LCC PS3611.R84 (ebook)
   | DDC 811/.6—dc23/eng/20221223
LC record available at https://lccn.loc.gov/2022057023
LC ebook record available at https://lccn.loc.gov/2022057024

The National Endowment for the Arts, the Los Angeles County Arts Commission,
the Ahmanson Foundation, the Dwight Stuart Youth Fund, the Max Factor Family
Foundation, the Pasadena Tournament of Roses Foundation, the Pasadena Arts &
Culture Commission and the City of Pasadena Cultural Affairs Division, the City of
Los Angeles Department of Cultural Affairs, the Audrey & Sydney Irmas Charitable
Foundation, the Meta & George Rosenberg Foundation, the Albert and Elaine
Borchard Foundation, the Adams Family Foundation, Amazon Literary Partnership,
the Sam Francis Foundation, and the Mara W. Breech Foundation partially support
Red Hen Press.

First Edition
Published by Red Hen Press
www.redhen.org
Printed in Canada

Acknowledgments

My gratitude to the editors of *About Place, Adanna Poetry Review, Alaska Quarterly Review, Alternative Field and Avenue 50 Studio, Catamaran Literary Reader, Poemelion, New Ohio Review, Red Wheelbarrow, San Diego Poetry Annual, SWIMM*, and *The 2 River Review* for publishing some of these poems or a version of these poems.

A version of "Still Life, Origami" is published in the anthology *In Isolation* (Alternative Field and Avenue 50 Studio, 2020).

Versions of "Still Life, Origami" and "Still Life, Yellow" are included in the artist's book *Still Life* (Bonnie Saland and Lisa C Krueger, 2023)

A version of "Security" is published in the chapbook *history beyond honeysuckle* (dancing girl press, 2023).

Thank you greatly to the editors of *Healthcare Professional Writings: Loss, Grief, Resilience and the COVID-19 Pandemic*, for including some of the poems and the epilogue in their anthology.

Thank you to the kind poets whose response to some of these poems grounded and guided me: Jane Hirshfield, Brian Teare, Jim Moore, Vieve Kaplan, Elline Lipkin, Beverly La Fontaine, Sally Krueger-Wyman, Craig Morgan Teicher, Kate Gale. Thank you to everyone at Red Hen Press, especially Kate Gale and Mark Cull, for their generosity and vision. Thank you to my steadfast and dear friends and family—you give me heart. Bob and Sally: always, my shining stars.

To my loves

Heritage

I invent Gabrielino women the way
I invent grandmothers I never knew—

my hands digging into land
that other hands have excavated.

Tongva. Hahamog'na. Who forged
willow domes. Carved bowls from stone.

The women before me knew
which flowers were delicious,

which could heal. Some were shaman
who shape-shifted, drank toloache.

I tend stolen soil, claimed by Spain,
sold by Mexico, repurposed and renamed

by Anglos with titles like Eaton. My home
is called Pasadena, Crown of the Valley,

souvenir word from a Chippewa tribe
that never lived here.

In my mythology of comfort, my map
for dark days, the women

are telling stories, arguing, singing
with percussion rocks and too much wine;

mothers of mothers of mothers
writing poems no one will see,

lacing flowers in their hair. Flame-keepers.
Women eager to speak

despite what comes after, daring history
in each small act,

foraging and digging for what will heal.
Burying their love in the earth.

Contents

II

III

IV

Floriography Child

A woman can't be, until a girl dies. . . .
I mean the sprites that girls are,
so different from us,
all their fancies, their illusions,
their flower world, the dreams
they live in.
                    —CHRISTINA STEAD

Where does this tenderness come from?
                    —MARINA TSVETAEVA

And yet the dream of the free body
doesn't go away. It buzzes in the air.
It smells of honey.
                    —OLIVIA LAING

I

THE TREES ARE BURNING

I.

I watch closely
her eyes
close I close

shutters against
bloom light
unfolding slowly

my daughter
ill again the disease
sharpens its image

comes into focus
at first it's a star
then a black hole

or light refracting
inside a lens, ghosting
its own brilliance

my daughter
the photographer
in a dark room again

camera's black bulk
waiting for her
she captures

torn petals
yellow stains
piston on asphalt

spindle and smoke
of trees in flames
our ridge is burning

she dodges and burns
in a light room
in bed
she needs
the dark I sit
in darkness

listen to lisp
of bougainvillea
falling;

leave to sweep
blooms that elude
like smoke kiss.

II.

Pulling weeds
at sunset above
my mother's ashes

forget-me-nots
vanish sky knits
its pink blanket

every way
I turn
ashes fall

in the pink
abyss a rain
of embers

III.

In birdsong
and traffic
I hear my mother

I listen to falling
blooms she is
alive to me

even as darkness
silences;
Mother! Mother!

Do you hear!
my daughter cries out
when she is ill

can't hear my reply
rocking rocking
we are

rocking I touch my
daughter's face
here I am

flare of spring fires
in the silhouette of trees
Mother!

Mother! wanting
our mothers
my daughter's body

lets go like spring's
almond blooms,
Mother be here

IV.

Barefoot on spears
of bleached grass
brown desiccation

of yard
to plant seeds
in a blister of drought

even when she's ill
she wants to plant
Oh, our sunflowers

toppled! Focus:
she caresses
each fallen bloom

V.

Shelter her:
shelter shelter
her she she shelter

her she she toppled
from heat she
toppled

illness burning through
like sun
through clouds

can't stand
in swelter my
daughter can't stand

come in
come in
come in

want the garden
come in
LEAN on me

LEAN LEAN LEAN
on me she can't
leave the couch

in and out like moon
in a storm her mind
bloodless

VI.

She asks for her basket
of seed packets beans
squash carrots

lying on the couch
I think of trees
felled in the fire

she reads planting
directions slowly
her mouth thick

with effort closing
her eyes. The basket
rises and falls.

VII.

can't catch

her breath/I can't

catch my breath/almost

breathe/breathe/breathe

I say/my daughter says

don't say that/I am

didn't realize I said it

aloud/she heard

on the couch/trembling

might pass out/might

could you come close/could

you touch me? she says

I lean over/hold her

whisper don't worry

don't

worry/don't

angry at me

I am not/stop it

oh/I was

talking

to myself

VIII.

Nothing to do,
my daughter says,
maybe she's better,

get on with my own
life: light candles
in the kitchen,

drink wine
too early;
DISTANCE, she texts.

DISTANCE REPAIRS.
She sends photographs
of seared limbs

in hills of open flame:
trees stand
through conflagration

IX.

Changes her mind.
Mother, something
you can do

holding forth
her largest lens
the terror

burning
we walk
below hills

aflame to groves
where ocean light
splinters eucalyptus

ablaze in pink
smoldering
closing in

like dreams
I can't release
Let go, my daughter

says, Mother
be
a tree

cauterized
stripped
hollow

burrow
sway
grow:

Floriography of a Birth

Daisies for innocence, roses
for love—everyone speaks

a little flower, lexicon
of forebears. Dahlias

for dignity, rosemary
for remembrance:

not ill but daffodil, born
under summer's golden moon.

I bargained for her!
Anything, I whispered,

on my knees in the garden,
leaves falling as I dug past light.

Hardship. Illness—
I said it, I said it—

Sunflower

Rapture of seed and fire—
third day after birth,

I take her to the garden,
announce myself:

I grew this for you.

Lifting her toward miracles
of suns bending—alleluia—

my August runner beans,
planted too close,

twining around each stalk.
Twist of fate.

Brilliant shack of sun-shock
already in prayer—couldn't

carry the weight of themselves—
just born, fading.

Hold Your Head Up

Your daughter acts spoiled, the teacher says, like she's used to having things done for her. Other children finish the projects and move on, but she puts her head on the table. Says she needs more time.

My daughter is five. My daughter sometimes has trouble doing things as fast as other people—her big brothers, for example, or her whole family. Hurry up! we call out to her. She who once acted precocious, who walked and talked and went everywhere with books at twelve months. See her now. Her body so slow.

No one has told me that my child has an illness without a cure. I have not yet been brought to my knees. I still live on dreams.

Sometimes, my daughter says, my whole body feels heavy but my head is light and I can't think. Sometimes at school she rests her head in her hands. Mrs. C. chides her. What, is your head too heavy for you to hold it up?

CAMELLIA, BRUISE

can't lift her head
wake up honey
school calling
is she faking

camellias by her
window opening
themselves like
unabashed valentines

they bruise   they bruise
bring her one sasanqua,
dark pink with gold
on her pillow

Growing Iris

I divide them the September
my daughter becomes ill.

Eight years old,
trying to dance

among basketball rebounds
of brothers keeping score:

I am busy. I turn over earth
for iris, my slender producer.

Who doesn't ask for anything.
Whose silken scarves smell

like jelly beans, spring, dreams.
Who dances.

Third Grade, Rumors

My daughter misses a lot of
school. Her body hurts—joints,
neck, back, abdomen—she is
exhausted all the time. Puffy and
pale. Not hungry but gaining
weight.

A journey begins. Morning to
late afternoon, doctors, labs,
clinics. I earnestly initiate a chain
of correspondence with teachers
that will go on for the rest of her
childhood. Sally is not well today.

I pick up, then return, missed
class and homework packets.
Pack lunches that never go to
school. Schedule doctors' and
testing appointments, call for lab
results, recognize each
receptionist by the sound of their
voice.

The mothers are talking. A
rumor spreads that I indulge
my daughter since she is my last.
That she acts out for attention.
That I want to homeschool.

My daughter and I spend so
much time in waiting rooms
that I imagine writing a book

about them. We play game after game of I Spy With My Little Eye until each of us knows all the answers. We have spied everything. At home, I listen to messages from doctors' offices. No messages about playdates.

On the down side, Sally's absences have left considerable

Sally has continued to have a difficult time with her health causing her to be in and out of class whether in the nurse's office or at home. She has worked hard to keep up with the class and has been a trooper about making up quizzes and work. For the most part, she has ___ined a positive attitude in spite of it all.

Dr Baufman 10/56 Ming down

FOREIGN LANGUAGE - SPANISH

Has acquired a solid vocabulary base	✓
___stood the relationship between subject and verb endings	NA
___ed previously learned material with new material	NA
___ to oral questions in Spanish with frequency and	NA
___t satisfactory mastery of material on the final	✓

to Sally's absences, it is hard me to evaluate her progress in 2 areas marked NA above.

Science

In spite of her absences,

Mon 10/1 Monday 10/1 woke up very tired + not well,
~~went to sch late~~ never went to sch', back to bed.
Called ████ re: recurrence of sinus + ear infec.,
prescribed Ceflex (Cefuroxime Axetil 250 mg)
for 10 days

on 10/8 10/2, 10/3, 10/4, 10/5, 10/6, 10/7, 10/8 in bed, weak +
exhausted.

Wed, blood test (mono @ Quest.
Resting, in bed until Monday, 10/15. On Augmentin.

Monday 10/15 Visit to Dr. ████ on 10/15.
Adrenals shot, recommended infusion starting 10/18
Tues 10/16 to tried school from 1 to 3, teacher told
her she'd have to take 3 tests on Wed,
came home overwhelmed + exhausted.
Wed 10/17 seemed to regress.
in bed rested slept until 11:15,
then ████ ████

Science

r to be in and out of class whether
...s and has been a trooper about
...attitude in spite of it all.
...f her absences.
...o miss so many days of school that last...

To Lavandula: Loss

Your allure like the lost self—
tender, recalcitrant,
never mistaken

for what you are not.

Open yourself, let
me cut you. I know
how. I watched

them cut my daughter,
pry her open, remove,
replace parts of her;

I will be gentle.

Injected, extracted:
if I strap you to a tray
and turn you upside down,

I will ask,
How do you feel?
But gently. Gently.

Let me lacerate.
Let me dry you,
release you in oils

and arrangements.

Blue Again: Plumbago

Summer's indigo mist

horizons the park

I walk toward

its sounds

of hide and seek

I'm fine now, go

after we watched sunrise

after the dark night

keeping each other awake

dark night of the dark night

I think I'm going to pass out

she had called to me

my daughter against me

for hours

stay with me

love oh love

staying with her

through the hours

plumbago surrounds

the park its sticky embrace

the color of sky

children are seeking

then losing themselves

Tea Time at the Playhouse

Let it be enough that she glimpses
what is wanton—sequin shawl

slung low across the back, old lady
body hunched in rainbow velvet—

everything bearing
its own weight—

for a moment, you are light.
The dolls are named Jasmine.

Amber. Ariel. They have not
been to the underworld.

No one has touched them
and told them not to tell.

No one has said,
It was all your fault.

This is spring, opposition
of fire. Party of mud cakes:

remember hunger. Party
of hose water: remember thirst.

These dolls look like dolls
you once believed.

Raise your acorn cup, toast
the forsaken world.

Checkout Line with Gladiolas

Renowned for the multitude
of their blossoms on stalks
that stretch toward heaven

from a wickered funeral stand:
weighed down by nodes.
Feed me! Feed me!

Each bud needing more
of what made them, even
when in full bloom.

I have seen glads languish
by a grave. I have seen them
sprout in a garden

then wither in a day. I have seen
boys grab them from a vase
to commence a fight.

I have seen my own self
seize a cellophane pack
of florid pink

with the sole intent
of cheering up
an ill child, seen myself

march into her room
with aggressive cheer—
pale moon of her face

on the pillow—ignoring
the petal memorial
of her bedside table.

PLAN

IF

- pale, can't talk / only stutters
- or shivers / cries, can't STOP
- head slumps
- tiny convulsions * or TWITCHES
- head slumps / eyes can't focus or eyes roll / body cold as ice
- DOESN'T RESPOND **THEN**

A recliner chair, ZIP INTO compression gear * electrolytes * SALT, hydrate, ice PACKS, more salt, Xtra meds, ask if 5 or 10 mg, IF no response, give 10.

- THEN IF NO RESPONSE, CALM, comfort, hold shoulders lightly, IF too sensitive bring head close to hers touch one foot lightly STAND but don't stare

DON'T

say oh god ! goddammit god please! DONT !
OR rock back + forth
OR make stupid small talk
OR cry
OR call 911 unless can't revive
or run away

Dandelion Mind

Be medicinal.
Resolute. If not careful,

you grow sour, bitter;
remain sweet. Golden

in hope. Buttery smiles.
Be secretive about work,

all the seeds you release
to the hieratic air. Others

will say, Oh look!
Once she was there.

Saguaro Cacti

A medicine woman in Ojai
sings in Lakota
over my daughter's body

then informs me
it's my sickness
not my daughter's

I swear off healers
until Shaman John
famous for hard cases

of mothers like me
who are parched
as cacti out Route 66

He instructs my daughter
to lie on his bed
which smells of whiskey

then places crystals
on her chest
tells me to leave

my energy
is interfering
I step out to asphalt

that melts my flip-flops
rise up with the Saguaros
symbols of motherly love

Away

We dip apples into honey for the sweetness of life; it is a new year, she tells me, this is what she does with loved ones. Red thread around her wrist. Heat pressing against us. There is no time to waste. I could begin again. We are sipping wine. My friend speaks of her art like a baby she nourishes. When she is with her work, the rest of the world falls away. I speak of my daughter's illness. She tells me I need to get out more; yet the world has fallen away.

II

Cycles

The land speaks to me
my better cousin
better half
better mother
than I ever
every plant every pod
every limb of tree
try try
even the earth
holds sorrow
layers and layers
of sorrow history
a lithosphere
of grief
eon after eon
of loss
finding expression
in an evolution
toward extinction
the way a species
of daisy
adapts to desert
by living
without leaf
how I want to be
unfettered
even seasons
are cycling
through personality
first moods
of ecstasy
now this

Make-Believe

So much will change the course of who we are. Today the children still laugh, look at us with open faces, as though we are gods.

Our gods are schedules and commitments. Our gods have nothing to do with the cast of light on the bowl of fruit or the smooth texture of someone's arm.

Our daughter is not well. She lies in the half-light of a long afternoon. Reads with earbuds; a river of words flows through her.

We are finishing bills and making appointments. We are driving through traffic, fretting over money and food.

We are making love and ignoring everything. We are opening up the medicine cabinet and staring at it. We are drinking too much. We are sleeping too much.

We are working too hard, we are cleaning all the time. Everything must be sanitized, everything could cause a problem.

We are bickering.

We are weeping.

We are no one's god.

Our daughter reads romance.

She loves the endings.

First Flush: Rose

You pull toy
of passion

with your broken
wheels of loss:

who else knows
all tongues?

My daughter wants
to make potpourri.

I carry blooms
almost spent

to her bed. She plucks
each slip of blush

with surgical care,
positions petals on a plate

I carry to a spot of sun.
Most scents are exiled

from our house
due to her disease,

but not this fragrance
of flowers dying.

THE TENDERNESS

We step outside, breathe smoke from
a fire we can't see. Pink neon lines the
ridge of our mountains, everything
cast in a strange glow. Heat became
an animal that lives with us, prowls
around the body, exhales against skin;
almost seductive. My daughter says
she needs to walk the garden. What
she does when she feels a little ill, feels
something coming on—an episode—I
see it. She slumps. Her face loses
expression. I call it a tour. Let's take
a tour around the plants. I imagine
the sensation, at the start, as a reeling
feeling, everything tilting, spinning out
toward darkness. What's going on, I
say to her. She can't talk, so hard to find
words, she tells me, everything becomes
confusing. Maybe the garden reminds
her of what continues. Leaning hard
against me. Keep going, she says. It's
her birthday, God. God. All the
years I have vowed not to be angry at
you. Walking toward a raised bed in
tangerine light, ash flakes beginning to
fall. The bud of a pumpkin has taken
a wayward path, scrolled up the edge
of a cedar plank, tendrils outstretched
toward heaven's utter silence. She lets
go of my arm, walks tenderly toward it.
Smiles. Cinderella's carriage, Mom.

After My Child's Episode, I Walk the Hills

Another tree felled,
its open grain
a stained bone:
I stumble in muck
of horse imprints
grown thick
from last night's rain,
wade through
yellow abandon
of wild mustard.
Imagine her gone.
No one to blame.
Blooms of crosses.

Diary by My Daughter's Bed

considering nature
as the cure for fear

Anne Frank wrote,
only then does one

feel all is as it
should be

glimpsing bare
branches then

early buds
of a horse chestnut

outside her annex
she never wrote

about autumn,
how a tree,

to survive,
releases itself

Portrait of a Mother

We are touring
the plots of dirt
where we sowed
corn and beans
three days ago,
the flush of early
heat in my daughter's
face. She sways
against me, her skin
ice-cold like
she might faint.
Maybe the illness
that has lain quiet
for a month—
no one says
remission—
is about to emerge.
She thinks we can
see sprouts. Too soon,
too soon, I can't
bear hoping for it.
I look away
at the vista of smoke,
swollen belly of ash,
don't say out loud
but think it,
Her life.
Hardscrabble.
Barren.
She is leaning
toward earth,
calling back to me,
Look closer.

Van Gogh's Mulberry

Once
I went to France,
looked through his
sanitarium window
to the woods where
he found himself
after a seizure
wrapped up
with a tree.
Five thousand miles
for permission.

STILL LIFE, YELLOW

When we walk out, light
has changed: each level

of the parking structure
is illuminated, miraged

in bands of lemon.
We pass a woman

in a wheelchair waiting
for her ride. She wears

a sunflower cap, gazes
straight ahead, motionless.

The doctor offered
good news, things look

fine, my daughter
can return in six months.

I vow to love
all over again.

RED DRESS

A hummingbird plunges,
misses my cheek, ascends
to her nest in the orange tree

where last year's final fruit
lingers side by side
with florets of spring,

their infant scent
a seduction, siren call
to romanticize

We walk among seedlings
below the silk
of her work,

hoping what we planted
hasn't withered
in the tidal heat

Get used to it,
says the woman
in a red dress

on TV,
our local
meteorologist

Every hummingbird
protects home even
when it costs life

My home is a fort
nothing can get in
that isn't already there

I want a center to hold
yet every poet knows
it never will

This bird's haven
dangles from a branch,
soft thumb of fate

Night Trees

A magnolia in my yard
has glossy sheaves
like a book I could read
forever, new chapters
at the tip of branches,
every narrative reaching
beyond itself:
trees have veins
yet no one can locate
their heart;
at night when water
courses through branches,
you can see limbs tremble
to pump sap,
if you wake
you can hear a beat.

Surviving Desire

When I was little I would wake in the dark to the sound of my parents fighting. Sometimes I heard my mother cry out, Oh! Sometimes in the morning she had a swollen face. Or a broken tooth. On those nights I pretended to be asleep. I pretended everything was alright. Suffering for what I couldn't do.

My friend says I need a T-shirt that says, Bad Buddhist. I am too attached to what I want life to be. I desire, therefore I suffer.

Sometimes I wake in the night to a voice that makes list after list of ideas, things I could do to make life better, make my daughter's illness go away.

What makes the engine go?
Desire, desire, desire.

Stanley Kunitz

Sometimes I think desire fuels my life.

My mother battled a horrific brain tumor. Six days before she died, she said to me, I think this is harder for you than for me.

I was shocked by her words. She was dying! I sat at her bedside, holding her hand. I was watching the clock. I had to make dinner for the kids. I was beside myself with anger and sorrow.

Don't go! I wanted to say. Go! Don't go! Go! Don't go! I think this is harder for you: those were her final words. She saw how desire consumed me. I could hardly bear it. She looked peaceful when she died. A tear slipped down her cheek. Oh, oh Mother. I kept thinking of childbirth, how the passages felt so alike. Once I had passed from her. Now she passed from me.

My Forgiveness

Yesterday I scraped
a car in the lot.
Its owner
came running—
the old shame.
I worked to be
a good girl
but failed.
Once I stole
a piece of lace
from my mother's
friend. My mother
made me
take it back.
I am sorry forever!
I said, crying,
certain there
would be
no forgiveness.
I still see
her walkway,
her trellis
of sweet peas
in the sun,
her face
as she bent down.

Lonely + Nature

I walk out my door
to the grasses

pledge my heart
caress the blades

let their slenderness
slice through me

Origami Night

Can't breathe, she says,
my chest hurts to inhale—

isolation flattens me.
My body folds into itself.

Breathe like this,
I say, slow ocean

sound of mouth,
air from my body

on the phone—
My head is light,

she whispers,
what if I pass out—

Breath is a raft,
I say; the phone

on my desk is dark—
little black box—

I catch my breath.
Twilight whisper

of a thousand cranes,
I hear her breathe—

I breathe—
we are breathing—

III

Trees Die Slowly to Survive

We swim in late light
near a line of redwood
spindled from drought;

my daughter's body
glides through water,
with ease, as though

all of her
was meant for this,
this deep water,

this almost dark,
her head lifted
above blackness,

the wake of her
rocking against me;
at ease; then evening's

west wind wandering
in the redwoods
that shift against

one another, rattling
like lost children
calling out.

The redwoods won't survive.
No evening mist arrives
to veil their limbs, each well

has gone dry. My daughter
photographs the grove's decline,
brings her lens up close,

so intimate with bark
that death becomes erotic, rivering
in fibrous plaques of disease

that embrace like bodies
desperate for love. Image to image,
I can't see change;

only the last photograph
holds out its darkened shield.
Yet here are the trees,

standing near as I watch
my daughter, a woman alone,
moving through deep water.

Avifauna

Peacocks
and parrots
are nesting
in our trees.
Absent traffic,
you can hear
your heart,
you can feel
earth vibrate.
Spangle and din,
dart and turn:
bird
on the unmown.
Birds' brains bulge
with neurons,
more per
square inch
than ours.
Morning feathers
mantle yards
like dew.
Shivs of divine.
Aqua and azure,
fire and coal;
gods don't change.

Shape of a Country

I park by the boarded-up
paint store, walk back

to her underpass where
she draws a map

in dirt with a stick.
I drive by you a lot,

I say; I worry.
She looks up,

her mouth a rose
of thin lip and gum.

This is for you—
I reach out.

She's younger
than my daughter.

Doesn't say,
Thank you.

Take care, I say.
Care, she replies.

SENSE

She is the age I was
when I gave birth.

Are her hands larger—
palm to palm,

we stretch ourselves.
Watch the other.

Someone will give in,
someone will say,

You have exceeded me.
Two doors away,

a mother calls out,
Come home!

The sky opens its trunk
of stars. Love scatters.

Repentance

thinking about god

and brutality, forgiveness
and summer harvest—

artemisia professing its glory
as though born

for this furnace,
this fury of history,

fire of caprice: tasting
like confession,

or piñon, or mother's skin,
bitter on the tongue:

Begin again

Begin again

Yard Sign

A corona of feathers
haloes the yellow finch

like petals
around pistil,

beauty in death
on my grass, screech

of red-tails above.
When my daughter

almost died, hawks
built unwieldy nests

in our pines; babies
cried at all hours

the way the living
always do.

Hands

I.

All night I comfort
myself with vows:
in the morning
I will dig new troughs
for potatoes.
I will move stones.
First one stone,
then more stones,
then all stones.

II.

My hands ache
to feel dirt.
The wild parrots
are calling out
to one another,
tree to tree—always
a lonesome flock.

III.

No one knows what
makes us belong.
Some nights, the past
roams around
like jasmine.

Real

A couple allows cameras into the NICU. Their baby, born ten weeks early, lies in an incubator. Unvaccinated, maskless, the mom contracted COVID. No one thought she would live. She smiles, weeps. I see her trachea scar.

We want everyone to know that COVID is real. It's actually real, says the father. He looks at the camera with wide eyes, he is crying.

Sometimes with my daughter's illness I feel the press of people's beliefs harden against my girl's life. I hear it in questions.

Has she tried going gluten free? Vitamin B? Acupuncture, reiki, infusions, glutamine, ketamine, sweat lodge, hyperbaric chamber, probiotics, fasting, chelation, grounding, vagal stimulation, aromatherapy, exercise?

Then the stone is thrown.

Volunteer work?

Maybe all my daughter needs is to think more about others, less about herself. Maybe if she took time to help others, she could emerge from a way of living that, the question implies, is in her control.

Once I asked a friend who was going through cancer treatment if there was something I could do for her. Yes, she said, you could get cancer too, so I wouldn't feel so alone.

Sometimes I wish people could have just one day—or one hour—of my daughter's life. I wish I could hear what they would say. It's real. It's actually real.

Street Blessing

Summers, we half-washed in sea;
nature, Mother said, was like home,

what we miss when we leave.
I am digging in dirt again, almost home—

the last day, she asked for the garden,
then said, I want to go home.

Eulogy: we're of the same source, each
seed another version of home:

her grave has forget-me-nots.
Dust of my mother, my home—

silt of all marvelous root—
I excavate for home.

Tangled life, verdant dreams.
I dream about the homeless.

Once I gave an offramp man my sweater.
Cars honked in a surge to get home.

Freed verse of my transient mind:
Barefoot. No shoes at home.

Dirt, like life, mother, home.
My daughter says she's going home.

The Ocean Is

Standing in our kitchen,
room of my life,
she says goodbye.
I cooked through
three childhoods.
She will live miles
away: separate.
What mothers
dream for a child.
We sheltered
so close
I could breathe
the loneliness,
could hear the illness
like sets of waves
during the night.
She is fine—what
mothers dream—
on the counter,
peaches and bread.

STATICE

shiver in the canyons,
slender fist of snake

hiss—dusk's yip
and wail of foxes—

waves' plume, quake—
lisp of brittle bloom

never ceasing
its lullaby—lulling—

bye—bye—what
survives. Wild plant.

Meadow. Everlasting
Calyx, Star of Passion,

Star of Death, its night
moving against us;

holding one another
in blankets of song;

Star of Memory.
Time. Canyon.

God. Lulling.
Bye.

I thought she might die. There were COVID patients everywhere, more coming in on stretchers. Sitting outside for six hours, waiting for her turn. My husband walking in and out, Our daughter needs help! I thought about my friend whose child died like this, no electrolytes left, a racing heart. Cardiac arrest. Stay, My Love. She couldn't hear. Stay, stay, stay, silently.

The admitting doctor said I couldn't be with her. COVID restrictions. I argued my way in: She has brain fog! She's almost unconscious! She can't understand a word you're saying! I rested in the small space by her foot.

Then to go forward in the disconnect— body pulling on socks—opening a door for the dog—another warm day. Talking to the heart, Don't break. Something wanting to loosen, slip away.

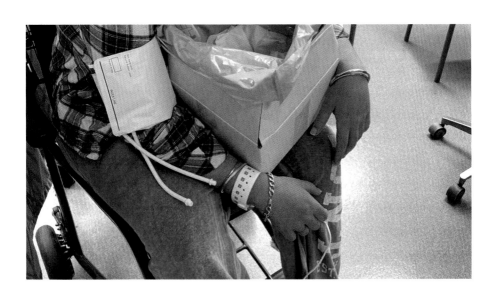

FLOWERS OPENING

Two girls emerged from the car
in tulle skirts scattered

with gold stars. Constellations
bobbed up and down.

We are shooting stars!
each called out to me,

running up the drive—
Shooting stars!

Their arms unfurled like flowers
opening. Waiting for them,

I unfurled. Stellar flare
on a Tuesday. Behind me,

the universe of exigent force
that owned me didn't exist.

The art of it:
lagoon of ruffled greens near a flag
of berries, jewel-blue and red.
The stall of tangerines,
burst of bright suns.
Simplicity of frame:
farmers standing behind folding tables,
customers in sneakers.
No illusion of separation in the line
that waits to pay for earth's bounty,
no one less than anyone else.
Some of us know each other's name.
Sue always gives me extra, since
long ago I helped her daughter.
Please no, I say. She asks about my girl.
Gives me news about family in Lebanon
and her Fresno farm: the drought means
they have to let some trees go.
Pressing into my hand a dark fig,
a cluster of lemon-sugared almonds.
Hon, your heart is so hungry.
Once I kept a platter of her peaches
on my counter, their bruise and juice
a soft feast on the tongue, a kind
of tenderness; she calls me Sister.

KNEELING NEAR LISCANNOR

Sorrow of clover on unmarked graves,
sorrow of the mass tomb: pushed forth,

across time, bone whelks jut from earth,
history emerging from its Famine pantry.

I see the skeleton of a child,
feel the surprise of devotion:

a mystic told me my daughter's Irish past
made her ill.

Anyone can walk to a sacred well, kneel
in granite grooves of those who came before.

I kneel for a friend back home,
killed yesterday while waiting in line,

shot in the back at Jack's. Sorrow of the burger,
the bystander, the kind cop; he lived near me.

I say his name. Officer Solano. Once he came by
for a false alarm. I'm ok, I said.

Let's walk around, you should feel safe,
he said, noticing my garden, shining

his light, talking about his kids
and the American dream.

IV

SECURITY

Days slipped through a sieve.
My imagination was exhausted.
Light was languorous. Outside the den,
a nandina bush performed as predator,
whisp of leaves, red berries dancing
around my paranoia. Every ten seconds
someone died, according to news feed—
we were supposed to stay inside.
On the security video, a racoon sorted
through a stash of candy I left
for delivery people. Racoons have long,
slender fingers, supposedly very sensitive.
I saw people drop wrappers
on the walk. I saw the racoon grasp a kiss
with two hands, unpeel the foil.
I hoarded takeout packets of soy
and ketchup, plastic forks, thin napkins
that did nothing for the mouth. I made
separate shelves for beans, cookies, chips.
I listened to a podcast about pandemic
hunger, one woman in a food line
said she couldn't afford snacks. Her kids
missed snacks. They were four and seven.
What do you mean, what snacks?
asked the reporter. Oh, fruit, the mother
said; they miss fruit. I had two orange trees
with so much fruit I learned to make marmalade.
I ordered two cases of jars to be delivered.
I ordered three cases of my favorite wine.
Fewer people began to die; I decided

to take bike rides, plant vegetables.
Rows of kale genuflected like mourners.
I found the racoon's narrow excavations;
roots were exposed, half-eaten,
everything upturned.

Blame

Most likely it's something she got from you, something you've carried with you most of your life, most likely something you got from your mother.

What my internist tells me.

Most likely there's nothing you can do about it now.

What does she mean? I read everything I can on the link between toxins and disease, how things can change the body's cell receptors. Things like arsenic, asbestos, BPA, TCE, Mercury. Mercury.

"There appears to be . . . alteration in the body's B cell receptors' signaling by low levels of exposure to mercury for the pathogenesis of autoimmune disease."

Vojdani, Pollard and Campbell, "Environmental Triggers and Autoimmunity."

My mind flashes to the tiny silver balls of mercury on our kitchen floor. I am about three, I am playing with them. They resist my fingers and roll away, I can't quite pick them up but I keep trying.

Don't touch! My mother's voice calls from far away, Don't play with it!

She leans down with a rag to capture the shards of our broken thermometer. I only want to help; there is something magic about the globes of silver all over our floor.

I think of my great-grandmother who sailed alone on a boat to America at thirteen. How did she make a life on her own? I think of my grandmother who was forbidden to attend art school; who died young.

Mother! Oh Mother! I heard my mother cry for her, sometimes, in the dark.

Some say time heals. Yet maybe the body holds what happens forever. The way earth holds us.

I.

In the photograph
my mother is ten;
she poses in a ruffled dress
and hand-me-down coat
that swallows her arms
the way shame swallows
people whole.

Lost in the oversize. Standing
near a clapboard porch.
She knows she is poor,
one of the poorest; her shoes
are too tight. Other children
tease her about the key
around her neck.

My mother makes drawings
of what she can't buy;
it will take years, and
thousands of dollars,
for her to learn that money
does not make her happy.

In the photo, my mother smiles
upward like the glamorous people
in magazines. She tapes sketches
of stars to her wall, studies them
before she falls asleep.

II.

My grandmother sews clothes
for my mother; she doesn't
need patterns, she has learned
to make things on her own
from what her mind can see.

My grandmother is a bank teller,
on her feet all day; tellers
are not allowed to sit. Only night
belongs to her. My mother
hears the machine, an animal
that growls in the dark.

III.

My mother's walls are rich
in the way my daughter's walls
will be, covered in desire.
My daughter will labor
over vision boards, collage
pictures of people and places
to help dreams come true,
what vision boards can do.

My daughter will stack magazines
by her bed, take scissors
to girls playing sports
with those beautiful bodies,
magnificent boys with interested eyes.
Picnics—dances—all the weddings—
cut out—

IV.

Sometimes, awake
with my own futility,
what I can't do for my child,
I picture the grandmother
I never knew,
bent over small light,
laboring. How many hours
to stitch ruffles?

V.

Standing, my mother crosses
her legs, an awkward pose,
perhaps one she has seen
in a star. Balanced forever.
Pinned to a wall.

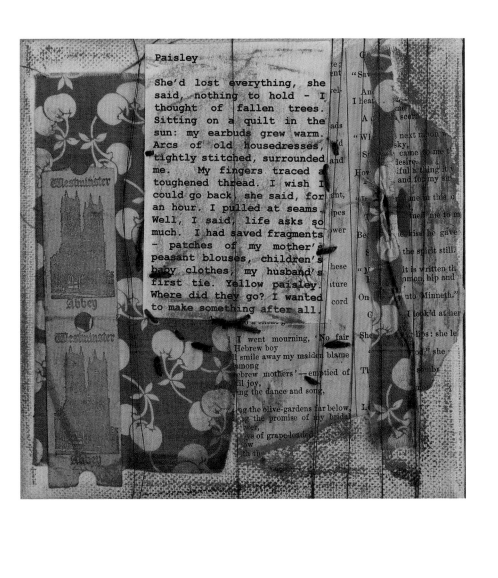

Paisley

She'd lost everything, she
said, nothing to hold - I
thought of fallen trees.
Sitting on a quilt in the
sun: my earbuds grew warm.
Arcs of old housedresses,
tightly stitched, surrounded
me.   My fingers traced a
toughened thread. I wish I
could go back, she said, for
an hour. I pulled at seams.
Well, I said, life asks so
much. I had saved fragments
- patches of my mother's
peasant blouses, children's
baby clothes, my husband's
first tie. Yellow paisley.
Where did they go? I wanted
to make something after all.

STATE OF MIND

Life with chronicity is a dream state, dusky and strange, never-ending. Beautiful things, wondrous things, are eternal: love, for example, or tumbling puppies. But not protracted illness, or disability, or psychic wounds that won't heal. Misery makes them chronic.

When I was twenty, a car of strangers ran a red light, broadsided my little sister's car, left her to die. She turned eighteen in a deep coma. When she woke, it took her months to swallow again, use the bathroom, focus. Head injury stole almost everything.

Coming to terms with chronicity, my sister was angry and mean for a long time. My mother absorbed the anger; mourned from it; grew depressed. Almost like a martyr, I thought to myself. Why would you let someone treat you that way.

I would never be like that.

Once my sister found a ring. Got down on one knee before my mother and said, Marry me.

My mother said Yes.

After my sister's accident, I worked for a while as an art therapist with TBI people—usually boys from motorcycles or construction sites. One man was a police officer. I enraged him. I am not in kindergarten! he roared at me.

Again and again he drew a small stick figure. Colored it over until everything was black.

His mother dressed him every day. Once she said, R___'s accident has been a blessing. Now we appreciate every little thing.

May I never have a thought like that.

What I said to myself.

What is endless? Paperwork, emails, laundry, dirty dishes. Headaches usually go away. Or fatigue: working too hard. Playing too hard. Temporary.

Chronicity alters temporality. For my daughter, one day of activity might mean three days in bed. A walk down the block can bring on extra meds. For pain. Or dizziness. Nausea. Brain fog. For a while, time disappears.

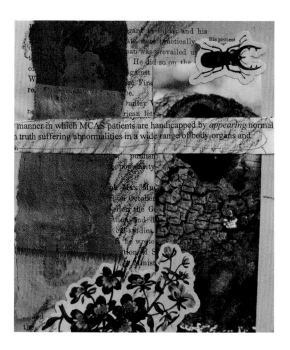

OUTSIDE THERAPY

Sitting across from someone closing
their eyes, I can't do this.

A canopy of oaks ribbons skin;
somewhere leaf blowers drone.

Leaning toward one who weeps,
a lizard by their shoe.

Feathers from a hawk-ravaged nest
make a mandala on grass.

Ninety degrees. A woman says, I left,
then panicked, went back.

Ninety-five degrees. A man shouts,
I don't know who they want me to be!

Out in the open, gestures look theatrical,
on stage; a squirrel pauses.

Late afternoon, someone whispers,
I am always afraid.

Acorns, feathers, strips of shed skin,
bone bits and seed stipple: what was alive,

what wants to live. All day with trees,
grove of the unbroken.

Internecine

A sparrow wrests her harvest
of dead things—acanthus leaf, lint,

brown furrow of oak catkin—
onto the wreath of our front door,

its plastic wands of lavender splay
around the promise of four eggs.

What every home is: tenuous.
We have stayed inside, burrowed

as hatchlings, paid people to leave
things on the porch: food, tissue, toys.

Watching too much TV, feeling numb
from the sight of kids wrapped in foil

on shelter floors or bodycam
replays of shootings.

Most days, stepping out,
we keep distance. Air sits

with its ghosts of smoke
from fires no one can stop.

In the house, little things have grown
nerve-worthy: dirty dishes,

the diaspora of our couch.
We fight. Then a morning comes

when we stand by the door,
hear the cheep of tiny creatures,

history's insistence on beginnings.
Ready to fall at our feet.

Getaway

In the afternoon we stroked
the bristles of an enormous pig,

discussed animals as sentient beings;
for dinner everyone ordered ribs.

Afterwards, we walked the dark road,
startled at a flash of white: owl.

Luminescent god. All night
something bloomed sweet.

At breakfast, people were ravenous,
ate everything;

Meat gives you energy, one said.
We strolled to corrals where hands

were saddling up the ten o'clock ride.
Everything glowed like a still life—

hangovers on faces, arthritis in fingers
that grasped the snakes

of weathered reins, blood flecks
where horse bits abraded gums.

Feed buckets, dung, rakes and boots—
some kind of fissured stage.

Myna birds taunted the tethered.
I wanted everyone to stop eating animals.

I wanted to say, You swallow their trauma,
yet who wants to lose family over food.

One had said to me, Come on.
Try the bacon. It's country.

Apostles

The succulent towered
above our yard
like an exceptional child,
staked its claim in shadows,
arms of darkness
perfect for afternoon drinks.
We cradled our highballs,
approached it with heads
bowed before an altar.
Chatted with lowered voices,
ignored the vortex of news
from a TV next door,
its buzz of death, protest,
hungry kids who couldn't learn.
When war came,
we changed the subject,
we only wanted
the solitude of our cactus.
Why it spindled
then withered
we didn't know:
twelve anorexic arms
fell to the ground
like a shattered earth star.
We stood in the sanctum,
a split space of silence
that embraced us.
We were haunted
by our loss,
without words,
we were yearning
to hear.

PAYMENT

She's asleep on the couch. I'm
washing dishes. What if we couldn't
afford this treatment. How can meds
cost so much. Who can't pay. Why
ok. Nothing ok.

Outside, my husband hands keys to
a man in a plaid shirt. We've sold
the van. We were going to see the
sequoias. Or a desert sky. Lie down
each night in the small space, forget
that we're growing old and our
daughter is ill. We bought it, parked
it in our drive for six months, sold it.

Come Back to Me

Memory fails
like a crumbling cliff

pebbles skitter
then the cascade

I walked my old beach
sand glittered with heat

surrendered like dry snow
each canyon barren

of the wild mustard
we used to pick

altered beyond recognition
the way some people look

after opposition
shadows of themselves

we would hike to where sky
fused with sea

wave at people camping in caves
carved by wind

some were naked
making love in the open

our cliff was gone
its wound of blue swelled

slender remains lay
as sandstone in shallow water

I couldn't remember
how to feel

change has stages
denial, anger, bargaining

then bursts of stone
roar of earth

BODY MIRRORS TREE

If you cut a limb above the node—
if absence swells what remains—

some trees won't repair
from necessary wounds

A woman slept
under a willow's arc

then under
a light's white ache

while surgeons cut
above the node

dreaming of doors
she walked through

to arrive, how they
sucked the air

like a baby gasping
for a breast

The woman was a mother
in many lives

even this life
under the light

while surgeons
lacerated

She was mothering
in her mind

remembering jacarandas
outside the hospital

that wept blue which
made visitors smile

Photo Album

You look nothing like that,
the child observes, turning
page after page of me.

Well, you don't look the same
as when I first met you,
I reply. But why, she asks.

I want to say life. I want
to say age, or death, but I
am not an open book.

I am a storyteller, I know
how to lie. I offer the old
narrative, It's late, let's play.

You be the baby, she says,
I'll be the mother.
You grow up and up, now

you don't look like a baby.
You're so big you're going
to heaven.

She flies her unicorn,
a spangle falls
at my feet.

When my daughter was first ill, I couldn't get past the sensation that no one was listening. I heard what people said about us: my child was stressed out or somaticizing. I was over-involved and high-strung. It seemed like I talked in a vacuum to doctor after doctor about brain fog, how it left my girl unable to speak, how plummeting blood pressure kept her motionless and in bed for days at a time.

Care no more for the opinion of others, for those voices. Do the hardest thing on earth for you. Act for yourself. Face the truth.

Katherine Mansfield

One famous Beverly Hills doctor said to me, Get hold of yourself or you'll give yourself cancer. Then he told my ten-year-old to watch her weight.

I was a ghost haunted by the Freudian specter of hysteria, wandering womb of the unanchored woman. Following me everywhere.

I have said to friends recently, I would like to be nonbinary. I would like to be they/them. I am so tired of gender constraints—I just want to be! Their faces are blank. Maybe they didn't hear.

Entirely

Leaving what was familiar—
        windows closed to heat
    and plague,

                    conditioned, purified—
            leaving the shore of she/her,
                  traveling toward they/them

in the way that trees
        lose leaves
   then rebloom, in the way

                  that saying I love you
            is not gendered, the heart
                being trans-

        formational

wanting language
        of a self
    unshackled

                  by label history
           speaking of freedom
                even this late

Freeway

Cement swans shadow lanes
in an eloquence of overpass—

interval of dusk for strangers
in commute, our collective

solitude its own darkness
through jams and delays,

our depths of sluggish
protraction, stops and starts

with opportunities for dream—
each of us growing anonymous.

No verdant fields or folds,
only the increment of time.

Illusions of separation dissipate
like exhaust. Valley of red light,

valley of white: weaving in
and out of ourselves.

Synovial

Membrane divides this from that—

      pith's insistence before fruit and mouth,

or horizon's stance against sky—

      partisan.

Some membranes are semi-precious.

      Water, say, or the brain—highly selective.

Skin is complicated. Seven layers

      between you and me

yet some days, one against the other,

      there are no barriers.

Connective tissue, envelope of self:

      two lovers embrace the lungs.

I breathe, you breathe—

      the filaments stir.

Granddaughter

Her body a whisper of girl, unlike
any I birthed—mine were sturdy,
solid; Germanic, my mother said.

Mama, am I fat?
my daughter used to ask.
This child pulls up pink ruffle

from hip to shoulder,
A mini-luau, I think to myself,
illogically, suddenly hungry,

thinking how I never believed
in starvation for beauty.
She watches me change.

My first bikini had pink hearts;
I didn't recognize my reflection.
After surgery, some women

can't look. Flowers on my suit
are gray. Sash of sundress, zipper,
everything falling away.

We are together in the mirror.
I always told my daughter,
Magnificent, you.

Floriography Child

I lose myself in Vuillard's berry pickers, lush bushes,
a tabby in the foreground whose head is the size
of a house. Sometimes I am cat, sometimes field.
Art saves me, I tell a friend. Well, join the club,
he retorts. Sorry, I answer. I know when to apologize.
I apologized to a waitress, once, when my dad
spilled martini on her; later I apologized to my dad
for the apology, then apologized to my mom
for the hurt the apology caused. He hit her.
I am sorry, I say, when I'm late, early, punctual,
overbooked. I apologize for saying too little,
too much, or for using the wrong tone.
Once before work I pushed my baby up the block;
a neighbor said, Well, aren't you gussied up?
Who are you? I didn't know. Once my supervisors
emailed me Dumb Blond Jokes; Sorry, not funny, I said.
Don't you ever laugh? they replied. Sorry.
I have apologized for being too helpful, not
helpful enough, for lacking affection, hugging
past the limit, loving in places where love
isn't allowed. Sorry, I've said, for brutal honesty
or lack of candor. Don't ever write truth,
one child commanded; another said, Jesus,
just say it! Sorry, I said, to each. On days I lose myself
in art, I imagine I won't apologize again, especially
not for dark views, insomnia, spiritual devotions.
Maybe not even for obsession with people's geology.
Vuillard's painting is languorous in wild fennel
and mustard, nature mingling with human form
as though we coexist. I live with longing. To all
who have left: I am sorry! Yet not for desire.

Song

Honey

of the body

amber

of the trees

I carry those

I have lost

inside

as song

a melody

courses through

keeps my heart

open

what if we

are the music

that moves

from voice

to voice

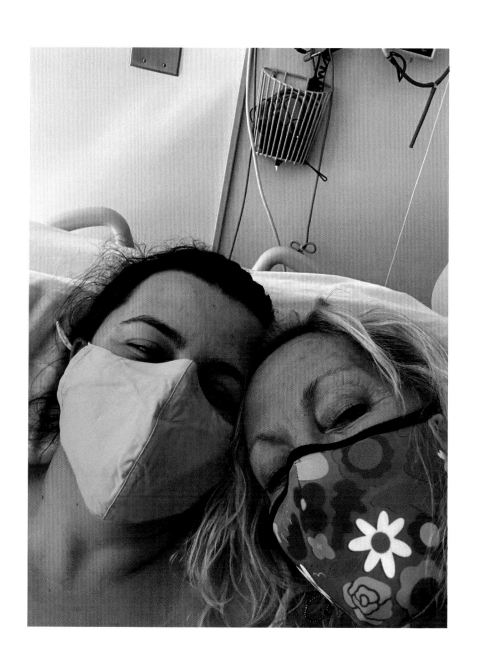

Epilogue: Chronic

The body doesn't care how wealthy you are, or famous, or intelligent. The body has more power. Illness reminds us that we are beholden. No matter our level of fitness or personal determination, our depth of spiritual connection or self-affirmation, the body wins. Illness, that unwelcome guest, strips away the black belt. There are only so many moves to make when facing a fever. A failing heart. A lung that won't expand. A cell that won't stop mutating.

Twenty-five years ago, when I was a young psychologist and my daughter was four, she became ill with an array of debilitating symptoms that no one understood: lethargy, swollen glands, an enlarged spleen; wrists, ankles, knees that hurt. Stomach pain. Doctor's visits circled around everyone's private fear of cancer. Repeated blood tests, physical exams, appointments with specialists offered no clarity. No one talked about dysautonomia, Ehlers-Danlos, Mast Cell Activation Syndrome, Hashimoto's, or Chronic Undifferentiated Tissue Disease—diagnoses that would be confirmed a decade later. Instead, doctors and educators talked to us about tolerance. The importance of resting, then getting back out in the world.

"How bad is the sore throat, really?" one teacher inquired. The administrator of her school told me my daughter was probably just depressed. Our pediatrician informed me he suspected an ulcer, and that he was sure my husband and I were putting too much pressure on her. A friend took me to lunch to tell me, "You should consider boarding school in the future. It would be good for her, and for you."

Illness is something every parent searches for and hopes never to find. Yet we always do, at some juncture of the journey—the flushed face, the fever in the night, the listless body. Is our baby alright? Our child? Our teen? It can't be too serious, right? It has to pass, right?

Carry on. Health, for many—if they are lucky—feels like a right. An entitled wealth, even. Illness, then, can seem an aberration. A mistake. I have noticed that people often feel sorry for the sick child—the first grader who misses a week of school for the flu, the high schooler with mono who can't go to prom. But the ill child elicits different feelings. The ill child alludes to life's mysteries, the larger powers of nature or god or circumstance, depending on personal belief, that we can't comprehend or control. The ill child reminds us of what doesn't blend in with the lights and glitter of yearning and hope. The ill child reminds us of darkness.

Throughout my years of work as a therapist, I have been deeply affected by the isolation of illness. How often people who endure some of the most painful experiences in life—depression, panic, phobia, paranoia—feel completely alone in their suffering. Connection and community are necessary to healing. Yet we abandon one other.

The pandemic opened my heart even wider to the ways in which we suffer. People sought therapy for problems they never expected to encounter: issues related to family, friends and community, questions about personal identity or sense of self. The global health crisis required many to rethink beliefs and life choices. Most significantly, the pandemic eroded a fundamental resilience that many took for granted, leaving them feeling less capable, often less hopeful, about their future.

Today, many of my daughter's health challenges from dysautonomia resemble those of COVID long-haulers: exhaustion. Tachycardia. Joint pain. Sleep issues. Digestion issues. Brain fog.

Her brain fog is my nemesis. I can hardly bear it, some days, how suddenly she can't think straight or speak clearly—or at all. Brain scans show a fifty-four percent reduction in cerebral blood flow velocity for her when she has just a mild episode of syncope, meaning there is barely enough oxygen going to the brain. We might be cooking together, or driving on an errand, or just sitting, and one of many triggers will elicit a change. Her autonomic nervous system is exquisitely sensitive.

Sometimes I think of it like a finely tuned, specialized race car. One minute my daughter is here, in this life: thinking, feeling, articulating her amazing self. Then she is gone. As though she left, all of a sudden, on an unexpected trip. Persephone.

One of the things I admire most about my daughter is what I think of as her philosophy of endurance. Sometimes she is so ill that she is barely conscious. Then her body finds its way back; she picks up where she left off and goes on. I think of her as a tree in the wind. She bends but does not break. Keeps growing.

My daughter spends much of her life alone: resting, recovering, gathering strength to be in the world, as health allows. She is an incredible artist and writer. She helped create a support network for people with dysautonomia and has a wonderful online community of friends. "Together, alone," she says to me about her life.

There is so much to come that we can't predict. The pandemic brought change and uncertainty to most of our doorsteps. My daughter has learned to navigate the pitfalls and pain of life with an attitude of grit and expectation: she gets through difficult episodes to anticipate better times.

I wish for everyone that personal challenges and world challenges might open doors to new ways of seeing and being. I wish that the demands of this moment in history might connect all of us to a larger purpose—and to each other.

Images

Notes

The following books and articles were instrumental to the creative process in relation to chronic illness, dysautonomia, and POTS:

BOOKS

1. Afrin, Lawrence B., *Never Bet Against Occam: Mast Cell Activation Disease and the Modern Epidemics of Chronic Illness and Medical Complexity* (Bethesda: Sisters Media, LLC, 2016).

2. Bernhard, Toni, *How to Be Sick: A Buddhist-Inspired Guide for the Chronically Ill and their Caregivers* (Somerville: Wisdom Publications, 2010).

3. De Wild-Scholten, Mariska, *Understanding Histamine Intolerance and Mast Cell Activation* (www.histmaine-intolerance.info, 2013).

4. Freeman, Kelly, Goldstein, David S., and Thompson, Charles R., *The Dysautonomia Project: Understanding Autonomic Nervous System Disorders for Physicians and Patients* (Sarasota: Bardolf and Company, 2015).

5. Grubb, Blair P., and Olhansky, Brian, *Syncope: Mechanisms and Management* (Malden: Blackwell Publishing, 2005).

6. Jacqueline, Ilana, *Surviving and Thriving with an Invisible Chronic Illness* (Oakland: New Harbinger Publications, 2018).

7. Masterman, Genny, *What HIT me? Living with Histamine Intolerance* (info@histamineintolerance.org.uk, 2013).

8. Rhum, Jodi Epstein, and Blitshteyn, Svetlana, *POTS: Together We Stand Riding the Waves of Dysautonomia* (Jodi Epstein, SHARED PEN Edition, 2011).

9. Walker, Amber, *The Trifecta Passport: Tools for Mast Cell Activation Syndrome, Postural Orthostatic Tachycardia Syndrome and Ehlers-Danlos Syndrome* (Kindle Direct Publishing, 2021).

10. Walker, Amber, *Mast Cells United: A Holistic Approach to Mast Cell Activation Syndrome* (Kindle Direct Publishing, 2019).

ARTICLES

1. Ballestar, Estaban, "Epigenetics Lessons from Twins: Prospects for Autoimmune Disease," in *Clinical Reviews in Allergy & Immunology*, 39, 30–41 (2010).

2. Bayles, Richard, KN, Harikrishnan, Lambert, Elisabeth, Baker, Emma K., et al., "Epigenetic Modification of the Norepinephrine Transporter Gene in Postural Tachycardia Syndrome," in *Arteriosclerosis, Thrombosis, and Vascular Biology*, 32, 1910–1916 (2012).

3. Jeffries, Matlock A, and Sawalha, Amr, "Autoimmune Disease in the Epigenetic Era: How Has Epigenetics Changed Our Understanding of Disease and How Can We Expect the Field to Evolve?" in *Expert Review of Clinical Immunology*, 11 (2015).

4. Sieverling, Carol, "Paul Cheney's NIMH (Neurally-Mediated Hypotension) Treatment Protocol for Chronic Fatigue Syndrome," www.prohealth.com, 2002.

5. Vojdani, Aristo, Pollard, K. Michael, and Campbell, Andrew W., "Environmental Triggers and Autoimmunity," in *Autoimmune Disease*, 798029 (2014).

Lisa C. Krueger, PhD, MFA, is a clinical psychologist. Her poems have appeared in various journals, including *Alaska Quarterly Review*, *Ploughshares*, and *Prairie Schooner*, and with Red Hen Press. She has published articles on the creative process and parallels between poetry and therapy, as well as interactive journals for girls and women. Recent poems have been included as finalists for the Catamaran Poetry Prize, the Red Wheelbarrow Poetry Prize, the New Ohio Review Prize, and the Pushcart Prize. She maintains a therapy practice with subspecialties in health psychology, women's issues, and writing therapy. She lives in Pasadena, CA. *Floriography Child* is her fifth book of poetry.